TABLE OF

ABOUT YOUR ADVENTURE

YOU live in one of the world's most powerful cities. Will you experience ancient Rome during Julius Caesar's rule, Emperor Nero's reign of terror, or the Visigoth's sack of the city?

In this book, you'll explore how the choices people made meant the difference between life and death. The events you'll experience happened to real people.

Chapter One sets the scene. Then you choose which path to read. Follow the directions at the bottom of each page. The choices you make will change your outcome. After you finish one path, go back and read the others for new perspectives and more adventures.

YOU CHOOSE the path
you take through history.

The ancient Romans spoke Latin. Many English words come from Latin.

YOU CHOOSE™
BOOKS
Historical Eras

Ancient Rome

An Interactive History Adventure

by Rachael Hanel

Consultant:
Richard S. Williams
Associate Professor of History
Washington State University, Pullman

CAPSTONE PRESS
a capstone imprint

You Choose Books are published by Capstone Press,
151 Good Counsel Drive, P.O. Box 669, Mankato, Minnesota 56002.
www.capstonepress.com

Copyright © 2010 by Capstone Press, a Capstone imprint.

Printed in the United States of America in North Mankato, Minnesota.

092009
005618CGS10

Library of Congress Cataloging-in-Publication Data
Hanel, Rachael.
    Ancient Rome: an interactive history adventure / by Rachael Hanel.
    p. cm. — (You choose: historical eras)
    Summary: "Describes the life and times of ancient Rome. The readers' choices reveal the
historical details of life from the perspectives of a wealthy Roman man, a young Roman woman,
and a peasant" — Provided by publisher.
    Includes bibliographical references and index.
    ISBN: 978-1-4296-3416-8 (library binding)
    ISBN: 978-1-4296-4865-3 (paperback)
    1. Rome — History — Juvenile literature. I. Title. II. Series.
DG77.H32 2010
937 — dc22
                      2009028153

Editorial Credits

Megan Peterson, editor; Veronica Bianchini, book designer; Wanda Winch, media researcher;
    Laura Manthe, production specialist

Photo Credits

Alamy/Lebrecht Music and Arts Photo Library, 59, 76, 89; The Art Archive/Museo Capitolino Rome/
Alfredo Dagli Orti, 57; The Art Archive/NGS Image Collection/H.M. Herget, 52; Art Resource, N.Y./
Giraudon, 46; Art Resource, N.Y./Réunion des Musées Nationaux, 12; The Bridgeman Art Library
International/Giraudon/Lauros/Private Collection/Gravelot, Hubert, 28; The Bridgeman Art Library
International/©Guildhall Art Gallery, City of London/Armitage, Edward, 67; The Bridgeman Art Library
International /©Look and Learn/Private Collection, 34; The Bridgeman Art Library International/©Look
and Learn/Private Collection/Embleton, Ron, 99; The Bridgeman Art Library International/©Look and
Learn/Private Collection/Jackson, Peter, 41; The Bridgeman Art Library International/©Look and Learn/
Private Collection/McBride, Angus, cover; The Bridgeman Art Library International/Photo ©Christie's
Images/Brindesi, Jean, 90; The Bridgeman Art Library International/Private Collection/Imperial Rome:
Circus Maximus, Sorrell, Alan (1904-74), 17; The Bridgeman Art Library International/Private Collection/
Valda, John Harris, 6; Capstone: Compass Point Books/Chris Forsey, 64, 70, 83; Getty Images Inc./Time
Life Pictures/Mansell, 75; The Granger Collection, New York, 100; Mary Evans Picture Library, 18, 24, 79;
Mary Evans Picture Library/Edwin Wallace, 31; Shutterstock/polartern, 105; Shutterstock/Rostislav Glinsky,
102–103; SuperStock, Inc./Fine Art Photographic Library, 55; SuperStock, Inc./SuperStock, 37, 49

City at the Center of the World

The era of ancient Rome lasted from about 753 BC to AD 476. Life in ancient Rome was filled with excitement, battles, and hardships.

Ancient Rome can be divided into three time periods. In the very beginning, a series of kings ruled the city and nearby lands.

In about 500 BC, Rome entered its republic era. Rome grew to include neighboring territories called provinces. During the Roman Republic, two ruling men called consuls made the decisions. Consuls served one-year terms and shared power. A group of upper-class men called senators helped the consuls make decisions.

Turn the page.

Rome was an empire from 27 BC to AD 476. During this time, the Roman Empire grew quickly to include most of Western and Eastern Europe, Northern Africa, and parts of the Middle East. For much of that time, emperors ruled the empire from Rome.

All business took place in the center of the city, which was called the Forum. In this bustling town square, politicians made speeches to the public. People gathered to buy and sell goods.

In many ways, Rome was ahead of its time. A complex highway system took people from place to place. Aqueducts brought water from rivers to public baths and private houses. Beautiful marble and stone buildings filled the city.

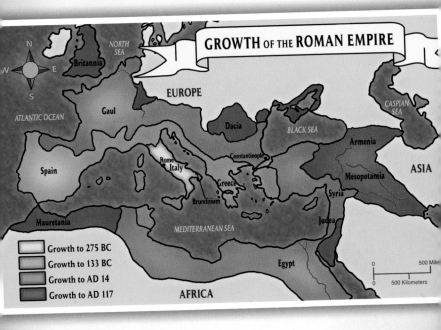

GROWTH OF THE ROMAN EMPIRE

Growth to 275 BC
Growth to 133 BC
Growth to AD 14
Growth to AD 117

A large army helped make the Roman Empire one of the largest and most powerful empires in history. Many of the battles were brutal and violent. Sometimes the Roman Army suffered large losses.

Turn the page.

At the center of Rome were its people. When the empire was strong, hundreds of thousands of people lived in Rome. Romans enjoyed art and theater. They gathered in large arenas to watch bloody gladiator fights and exciting chariot races. Many people went to the bathhouses to swim or relax in hot and cold baths.

Wealthy citizens filled their homes with paintings and sculptures. Their homes had kitchens, bedrooms, and living areas. Poorer Romans lived in crowded apartments. These apartments often collapsed or caught on fire.

Rome was a mix of citizens, noncitizens, and slaves. At first, only people born in Rome could become citizens. As Rome grew, more people were granted citizenship. Citizens had legal rights and could enter politics. The powerful general and politician Julius Caesar is ancient Rome's most famous citizen.

Noncitizens had fewer rights. They were born outside of Rome and could not take part in politics. Slaves had no rights at all. They lived under the control of the wealthy class. But slaves were sometimes set free and could even buy their own freedom.

For everyone, life in Rome could be hard at times. People died from disease and starvation. Many women died during childbirth.

But it was also exciting to live in one of the world's busiest cities. Life could offer adventure and power. Each person's experience was unique. What will your life be like in ancient Rome?

11

✦ To experience life as a wealthy Roman man during the late republic, turn to page **13**.

✦ To explore life as a Roman woman during the early empire, turn to page **47**.

✦ To live as a poor Roman citizen as the empire weakens, turn to page **71**.

Julius Caesar was elected consul in 59 BC.

CHAPTER 2

Witness to History

It's January 49 BC. Trouble is brewing in Rome. Former consul Julius Caesar has spent the last nine years leading his army in the western part of the republic. Caesar's army has conquered a large territory called Gaul for the republic.

Pompey has also served as consul for the republic. Pompey and some other senators are jealous of Caesar's wealth and power. They ordered Caesar to give up his army and return to Rome. Caesar agreed to give up his army only if Pompey did the same. Pompey refused. If Caesar returns to Italy with his troops, a civil war will break out.

13

Turn the page.

Only upper-class men are allowed to serve in the Senate. They must first serve in the military. Then they must be elected as a quaestor by the citizens. Quaestors are a type of magistrate in charge of finances. After a one-year term, quaestors automatically enter the Senate.

Senators serve for life and have much power. They advise the consuls and approve legislation for public votes. They also pass official orders called decrees.

A Senate career is not the only choice for wealthy Roman men. The equestrian class is made up of Roman businessmen. They collect taxes, loan money, import and export goods, and build roads. For smart businessmen, there is money to be made.

⇰ To experience life as a Roman senator, go to page 15.

⇰ To explore the life of a Roman businessman, turn to page 16.

You are 30 years old and the first in your family to serve in the Senate. Some of the older senators are very conservative. They are afraid Caesar wants sole control of Rome. But Caesar has the support of Rome's commoners. In January 49 BC, he marches his army into Italy.

The Senate holds its meetings in the Curia, a building in the Forum. You are about to go home for the night when an older senator approaches you.

"The Senate needs your support," he says. "Caesar has started a civil war by marching his army toward Rome. The Senate wants Pompey to lead an army against Caesar. Will you come to our side?"

➤ To support Pompey, turn to page **18**.

➤ To support Caesar, turn to page **25**.

As a young businessman, you have many choices before you. Your father can help you start whatever business you would like to go into. But of course, he would like you to follow in his footsteps. Like many upper-class Romans, he lends people money.

Money lending would be a secure, stable business. You could help your father. And when he gets older, you could take over the business. There would be little risk involved.

But then you receive an offer from your friend Titus. He talks to you while you are watching chariot races at the Circus Maximus. This large building has many seats facing a center track. It's one of the most popular places in Rome.

The Circus Maximus could hold about 300,000 cheering fans.

"I'm going to invest in one of the racing teams," Titus says. "The green team is doing especially well. I will give them money to buy faster, stronger horses. Then I will receive some of the prize money if the horses win. Do you want to invest with me?"

Chariot racing is becoming more popular every year. Thousands of people fill the wooden stands of the Circus Maximus for each race. Prize money and treasures are handed out to winning teams.

→ To invest in a chariot-racing team, turn to page **19**.

→ To become a money-lender, turn to page **36**.

Pompey (on horse) left Rome before Julius Caesar and his troops arrived.

It is too risky to support Caesar. If he is defeated, you could lose your Senate seat. You choose to support Pompey instead.

Caesar and his troops march closer to Rome. You hear reports of how people in the countryside admire Caesar. "Hail, Caesar!" they shout.

"It is best that we leave Rome with Pompey," one of the senators tells you. "If Caesar takes power, what will happen to us?"

→ To leave with Pompey, turn to page **21**.

→ To stay in Rome, turn to page **23**.

Rome has four chariot-racing teams — the white, red, blue, and green teams. The green team is Rome's most popular team. You use some of your family's wealth to help the green team buy fast horses from Spain.

Your investment pays off. Chariot drivers on your team win race after race.

You put some of your winnings back into the horse stable. You buy more horses and hire someone to build lighter, faster chariots. Your team appears to be unstoppable. Your successful drivers can barely walk down the street without being mobbed by fans.

As you're walking to the stable, Titus rushes up to you. He's pale and looks worried. "Something terrible has happened at the stable. Come quickly!" he says.

Turn the page.

When you get to the stable, some of the horses are lying down in their stalls. Many are dead, and others are dying.

"What happened?" you cry.

"Our best horses have been poisoned," Titus tells you. "It must have been someone from another team."

"This is terrible," you say. "I'm not sure we can come back from this loss."

You've lost a lot of money. Almost every horse you bought is now dead. Maybe it's best to give up chariot racing. You could still go into the money-lending business with your father.

→ To go into business with your father, turn to page **36**.

→ To stick with chariot racing, turn to page **38**.

You travel by ship to Greece with Pompey, where he prepares his army. Caesar follows. Pompey's army is larger than Caesar's army. You are sure Pompey will win. You wait in Pompey's camp as the battle begins. Soon, one of Pompey's soldiers enters your tent.

"Caesar's army has defeated Pompey's troops!" he tells you.

"Is Pompey still alive?" you ask.

"Yes," the soldier says. "But he plans to flee to Egypt. He hopes to gain support from King Ptolemy XIII."

You go with Pompey and his supporters to Egypt. After many days, your ship arrives in Egypt. Ptolemy's men kill Pompey before he can make it to shore. Then, Egyptian soldiers seize you and those loyal to Pompey.

Turn the page.

"Our king supports Caesar," one soldier says. He locks up you and the other men. You wish you had never decided to support Pompey.

When Caesar arrives in Egypt, Ptolemy presents Caesar with Pompey's head. But Caesar is not impressed. He makes sure that you and Pompey's supporters are treated well.

Once Caesar takes full control of Rome, he forgives the senators who had backed Pompey. You return to your Senate position in Rome. But the republic is weakening, and Caesar has all the power. The men who supported him hold the most influence. And that group does not include you.

THE END

To follow another path, turn to page 11.
To read the conclusion, turn to page 101.

You stay in Rome while Pompey travels to Greece with his army. By the time Caesar enters Rome, he has the support of most citizens. Caesar and his army then follow Pompey to Greece.

You are walking in the Forum one day when another senator approaches you.

"Caesar has defeated Pompey," he tells you. "Now Pompey has fled to Egypt. He hopes the Egyptians will help him fight Caesar."

Things quickly turn sour for Pompey. King Ptolemy XIII has him killed once he arrives in Egypt. Caesar becomes sole ruler of Rome. He forgives those who supported Pompey, and you resume your Senate career.

Turn the page.

When Caesar returned to Rome, white horses pulled his chariot through the streets.

When Caesar returns to Rome, the celebrating begins. Plays, athletic contests, and animal hunts take place all over the city.

You enjoy the festivities as well. One day, you attend a staged military battle. Soon, the large crowd grows unruly. People begin to push one another. You try to get away from the crowd, but you are shoved to the ground.

"Help!" you shout. But no one hears you. In their excitement, the crowd crushes you to death.

THE END

To follow another path, turn to page 11.
To read the conclusion, turn to page 101.

To follow another path, turn to page 11.
To read the conclusion, turn to page 101.

24

You support Caesar. You think he's making exciting changes for the Roman Republic. He has increased its size by adding territories. He encourages people to settle these new lands.

Several weeks after entering Italy, Caesar makes it to Rome with the full support of the citizens. He defeats Pompey's troops in Greece and follows Pompey to Egypt. King Ptolemy XIII of Egypt supports Caesar. He has Pompey killed.

Caesar becomes the sole ruler of Rome, and peace returns to the republic. Caesar builds new roads, creates new jobs, and distributes grain to make sure that no one goes hungry.

Turn the page.

After a few years, the wealthy Roman senators look for ways to get rid of Caesar. Because Caesar is so generous to the commoners, the senators don't think he will protect their wealth. They also believe that Caesar wants to become a king and have full power over Rome.

It's true that Caesar does think highly of himself. He puts his image on Roman coins. He wears the finest robes. He insists on public celebrations of his birthday and the anniversaries of his military victories.

You arrive at the Senate house one morning. Appius, another senator, approaches you. "What do you think of Caesar?" he asks.

"I think he has done some good things," you say. "But I don't like the way that he is always the center of attention."

"Exactly!" Appius says. "It can only get worse. Some senators worry that Caesar wants full power over the republic. He might get rid of the Senate. Some of us have a plan to stop him."

You look at Appius. "What do you mean?"

Turn the page.

Brutus and Cassius both supported Pompey and were later forgiven by Caesar.

"Senators Marcus Brutus and Gaius Cassius have hatched a plot to kill Caesar. But we need help. Will you join us?"

If you help kill Caesar, you might find favor with the powerful senators. With their support, you could have a long and respected Senate career. But if the plot fails and Caesar lives, everyone involved would be put on trial. You might be put to death for treason.

→ To join the plot to murder Caesar, go to page 29.

→ To say no to the plan, turn to page 33.

It is too dangerous to talk openly about the plot to kill Caesar. Appius invites you to his home.

"Caesar plans to leave the city on March 18 for his next military campaign," Appius tells you when you arrive. "We must kill him before he leaves the city. Caesar wants to meet with the Senate on March 15. The Senate chambers will be a perfect place for the attack."

"How can I help?" you ask.

"We need someone to distract Caesar. Then the rest of us will attack him."

The plan sounds easy enough. But if something goes wrong, you could be in serious danger.

→ To distract Caesar, turn to page **30**.

→ To back out of the plan, turn to page **33**.

On March 15, 44 BC, you arrive at the Senate early. Caesar enters the building. You and the other senators stand as he takes his seat at the front. Your role is to distract Caesar with a speech.

"Caesar, I beg of you. Please let my brother return to Rome from exile," you say. Caesar looks at you. He doesn't notice the other senators approaching slowly. "You have been so generous to those on the losing side of war. I ask that you extend that generosity to my beloved brother."

Caesar waves his hand at you. "This is not the time for this request. You can ask me another time. There is more important business to take care of today."

You move even closer to Caesar. "But please," you say. Then you pull on the shoulder of his robe. This move is the signal for the attack.

Just then, a group of senators rushes at Caesar. They stab him with knives. He raises his arms to shield himself but is defenseless against the attackers. After a few minutes, Caesar lies crumpled and bleeding on the Senate floor. He is dead. Those not involved in the attack flee the building, fearing that they might also be attacked.

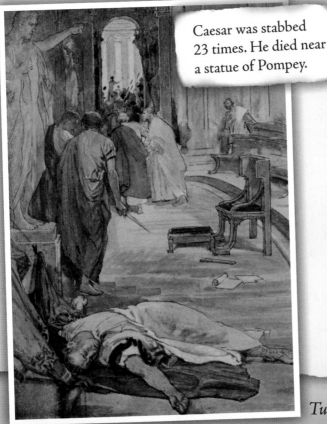

Caesar was stabbed 23 times. He died near a statue of Pompey.

Turn the page.

You and the other plotters thought you'd be considered heroes, but the murder angers many. Brutus and Cassius leave Rome. You flee to the countryside.

After Caesar's death, his adopted son, Octavian, takes power. He is joined by Caesar's friends Mark Antony and Lepidus. They vow to kill the assassins. After a few years, they are successful.

You are awakened one morning by a loud banging on your door. "Open up!" a voice shouts.

You throw back the covers and scramble out of bed. But it is too late. Several Roman soldiers surround you. You die as a result of your decision to take part in Caesar's murder.

THE END

To follow another path, turn to page 11.
To read the conclusion, turn to page 101.

You worry that the plot might fail. You don't want to make Caesar angry, so you decide not to take part in the plan. On March 15, 44 BC, you attend a Senate session that Caesar has called. As Caesar enters the building, you and the others rise to your feet in respect.

When Caesar sits down, a group of senators approaches him. They get closer and closer. Then you hear shouts. Caesar is being attacked! Caesar raises his arms to defend himself, but the senators stab him with knives. After just a few minutes, Caesar falls to the floor in a pool of blood. He is dead. You run away from the Senate, afraid the plotters might attack you next.

Turn the page.

Mark Antony spoke at Caesar's funeral, which took place in the Forum.

Soon, Caesar's adopted son, Octavian, takes his place. Octavian joins with Caesar's friends Mark Antony and Lepidus. They share power. Together, they kill everyone involved in Caesar's murder.

Octavian takes sole control of the Roman Empire in 27 BC. He changes his name to Augustus and becomes the first of many Roman emperors. Emperors have more power than the consuls did. They are not elected and hold the term for life. When an emperor dies, power is usually passed to a family member.

You continue a respected Senate career. But the Roman citizens now have little choice about who leads them.

THE END

To follow another path, turn to page 11.
To read the conclusion, turn to page 101.

People come to your father when they need money to start a business or buy property. He lends them money and charges interest on the loan. That way, he makes money for himself.

Your father teaches you everything you need to know. He sends you into the Forum, where you find people looking for loans. Other lenders are also trying to get their business. You have a lot of competition.

You meet up with your friend Lucius at the Forum. He also lends people money.

"I would like to expand my business into the provinces outside of Rome," Lucius says. "The residents there often need to borrow money to pay taxes. But I would like a partner. Are you interested?"

The ancient Romans gathered in the Forum to conduct business and meet with friends.

The idea of expanding your business appeals to you. But there is risk involved. Some of the provinces are poor. People there have a need for loans but may not be able to repay their debts. But if they repay their debts, you could make a lot of money.

➤ To invest in the provinces with Lucius, turn to page **43**.

➤ To continue building your business in Rome, turn to page **45**.

You help buy more horses, and the green team becomes strong again.

You enjoy going to the races. It's very loud at the Circus Maximus. Thousands of fans cheer for their favorite teams. Before the race starts, a procession marches onto the track. Horses, chariot drivers, dancers, musicians, and priests carrying statues of the gods parade in front of the crowd. People place bets on which team they think will win.

Just before the race starts, Titus finds you in the stands. "Our driver is sick!" he says. "He can't race today."

This is terrible news. Drivers compete in 12 races each day. Your team will lose money.

"Can we find another driver?" you ask.

"Not when the race is about to begin," Titus says. "You have experience with horses. Perhaps you could drive for the green team today."

You have often dreamed of driving in a chariot race. The best drivers win lots of money and become heroes. But most drivers are slaves or freed slaves. You are of a higher class. What would people think? Chariot racing is also very dangerous. Many drivers die while racing.

→ To drive for the green team, turn to page **40**.

→ To stay out of the race, turn to page **42**.

"I will race," you tell Titus. You and Titus run to the starting gate. You put on a sleeveless tunic and a leather helmet. Then you climb into the chariot.

Titus wraps the reins tightly around your waist and hands you a knife. "Put this in your belt," he says. "Use it to cut yourself free if there is a crash."

As a trumpet sounds, the magistrate drops a napkin to signal the start of the race. An attendant pulls a lever, and the gates spring open. The horses rush onto the track, their hooves pounding on the dirt.

You slowly gain speed as you move through the pack. This is the most exciting moment of your life.

Most chariot races lasted for seven laps.

Suddenly the driver in front of you crashes into the side of the track. His chariot breaks into pieces. You pull on the reins and move your horse around the wreck. That was close! The audience breaks into loud applause. You have won the race.

You become one of the best chariot drivers in Rome. People cheer for you on the street. You become rich beyond your wildest dreams.

THE END

To follow another path, turn to page 11.
To read the conclusion, turn to page 101.

"It is too dangerous," you tell Titus.

"Then I have no choice. I must drive for the green team." Titus runs to the starting gate before you can stop him.

Your stomach churns as you watch from the stands. A trumpet sounds, and the magistrate drops his napkin to start the race. When the gates open, the horses gallop onto the track.

The drivers round the first corner. Crash! Several drivers plow into one another. Titus is one of them. You rush down to the track.

"Titus!" you scream. But you are too late. Titus is dead. You wish that you had driven for the green team. Maybe then your friend would still be alive.

THE END

To follow another path, turn to page 11.
To read the conclusion, turn to page 101.

You and Lucius move into the countryside. You charge a higher interest rate on the loans. Everything goes well for a few months. You are able to take the money you earn and loan money to more people. You have a long list of people who owe you money. But your father has words of caution.

"Keep some of that money," he says. "Don't loan it all out. What if people aren't able to pay you back?"

But you become greedy. If everyone pays you back like they should, you will be richer than you had ever imagined. You build a large house and throw many dinner parties. Life is good.

Turn the page.

Soon, the provinces are in trouble. Crops fail, and people start fighting with one another. No one is able to afford the interest rate on their loans. The business you and Lucius started with such high hopes fails miserably. You are nearly broke. You can only hope that your father will help you get back on your feet. Otherwise, you will end your days as a poor Roman citizen, not able to afford the luxuries you are used to.

THE END

To follow another path, turn to page 11.
To read the conclusion, turn to page 101.

"The risk is too great to invest in the provinces," you tell Lucius. You have a small but reliable client list in Rome. You concentrate your efforts on the city.

After several years, your business decision pays off. You earn a good reputation as a fair and honest businessman. Your client list grows, and you even help other wealthy Romans loan out their money.

You buy a nice home in the hills overlooking the center of Rome. Each afternoon, you visit the public bathhouses. You attend gladiator contests and chariot races. For a wealthy Roman citizen such as you, life is very good indeed.

THE END

To follow another path, turn to page 11.
To read the conclusion, turn to page 101.

In AD 64, two-thirds of Rome
burned. Some Romans thought Nero
started the fire, but most historians
do not believe this to be true.

CHAPTER 3

Riches and Secrets

It is AD 62. Nero is the emperor of the Roman Empire. He is not a popular leader. For a time, Nero thought his mother and wife were plotting against him. He had them killed.

The Roman Empire is growing. It now includes Britannia in the North. Many Romans believe the empire is bringing culture and civilization to the rest of the world.

You are a young Roman woman of noble birth. You live with your family in a large house in the hills. You received some schooling in reading, writing, and math. You also learned how to sew. But you are now 15. It is time to marry.

Turn the page.

From birth, Roman women are under the control of their fathers. When women marry, control sometimes passes to their husbands. But wealthy Roman women who give birth to three children can gain their independence. These women are able to control their wealth. They can also own property.

Your family has chosen the man you will marry. His name is Gaius. He also comes from a noble family. He is a few years older than you are. With both of your families connected through marriage, Gaius will have more power in politics.

On the morning of your wedding, your mother, sister, aunts, and female cousins dress you in your home. You wear a simple white tunic, belted at the waist with a knot. On your head sits an orange veil. The women separate your hair into tufts and tie it with ribbons.

In ancient Rome, girls could legally marry at age 12 and boys at age 14.

After the wedding, you and Gaius feast with family and friends. Your family gives Gaius a dowry. This money will help you set up your household. Then you go to Gaius' family's house to live.

Turn the page.

After a year, you have yet to bear a child. Gaius has threatened divorce if you don't produce a son. Frustrated and sad, you speak to one of your female neighbors.

"What you need is a strong potion," she tells you. "I know a woman who makes one that works. Give it to Gaius, and he will become friendly again."

The use of potions is common in Rome. Women create drinks out of herbs and spices they grow in their gardens. Some even make and sell love potions.

➤ To decide not to use the potion, go to page 51

➤ To use the potion, turn to page 54

You decide not to use a potion. Before long, many husbands who drank the potion are dead, including your neighbor's husband. The woman who sold the love potion is put on trial and then put to death.

You are glad you didn't use the potion. You soon discover you are going to have a baby. When the day of the birth arrives, a midwife comes to your house with your mother and sister. They make you comfortable. The midwife places a hot towel on your swollen belly to ease the pain. The birth goes well. Gaius is pleased because you have given him a son. You soon give birth to two more sons.

Gaius is appointed to the Roman Senate in AD 65. He spends his days at Senate meetings or at the bathhouses.

Turn the page.

Your days are full, but you have time to relax as well. Each morning, a slave girl puts white chalk on your face and red ochre on your lips and cheeks. Then she curls your hair and piles it on your head.

Once you are dressed, you give the slaves their list of chores. "Clean the oil lamps and fetch fresh water," you tell them. Because you are wealthy, you hire a teacher to come to your house and educate your children.

Wealthy Roman women had slaves to help them get dressed and put on makeup.

One day, Gaius looks worried when he returns home from the Senate. "Some senators are plotting to kill Emperor Nero," he tells you. "They want Senator Piso to become emperor. He has promised to treat his supporters well."

"I agree that Nero isn't a great emperor," you say.

Gaius paces back and forth. "Some of the plotters are meeting tonight. Should I join them?"

As a woman, you cannot vote or hold office. But many women do advise their husbands on political matters. Gaius trusts your judgment.

➝ To encourage Gaius to join the plot, turn to page 56.

➝ To advise against the plot, turn to page 58.

You buy a potion and serve it to Gaius during dinner. A few hours later, he becomes very sick. He has a high fever. He talks, but his words don't make sense. You run to the neighbor's house.

"Something is very wrong with Gaius! I gave him the potion, and now he's very ill!"

By the time you return to the house, Gaius is dead. Many other husbands are also dead. The Roman magistrates find out. The woman who sold the potion is put on trial and executed.

You return to your father's household. Because you have no children, your family wants you to remarry. After a few months, you have many suitors. One in particular, Marcus, is gentle and kind. But a wealthy older senator, Decimus, also wants to marry you. Both Marcus and Decimus need children in order to continue their family lines.

➻ To marry Decimus, go to page 55

➻ To marry Marcus, turn to page 61

You marry Decimus and move into his household. You soon give birth to a son and two daughters.

After a few years, Decimus becomes very ill and dies. Because you are the mother of three children, you have earned your independence.

You must now choose what to do with your wealth. A few widowed and divorced women go into business, such as real estate. They also use their money to support artists, writers, and actors.

Some upper-class Romans hosted poetry readings at their homes.

➤ *To go into real estate, turn to page 64.*

➤ *To support the arts, turn to page 66.*

"With Nero out of the way, you will gain more power in the Senate," you tell Gaius. He agrees. You put on your best cloak and go with Gaius to Flavius Scaevinus' house. He is another senator who is in on Piso's plot.

Flavius is in a strange mood when you arrive. He has freed most of his slaves and given them gifts. He even signed his will. "Sharpen my dagger," Flavius tells Milichus, one of his slaves.

You gather with the other wives after dinner. "What is the plan?" you ask.

"The attack will take place tomorrow at the Circus Maximus," one of the women whispers.

At age 17, Nero became the fifth emperor of the Roman Empire.

When Gaius returns home the next day, you greet him at the door. "Is Nero dead?" you ask.

"No," Gaius tells you. "Flavius' slave Milichus reported his strange behavior to Nero. Flavius has been arrested. The plan is ruined."

You and Gaius are in danger. You know that Nero will kill those who plotted against him. But perhaps Flavius won't reveal your involvement.

❧ To stay in Rome, turn to page **60**.

❧ To try to leave Rome, turn to page **63**.

"The plan sounds too dangerous," you warn Gaius. "If the plot fails, Nero will kill everyone involved. Look at what he did to his own wife and mother. I think you should stay away from this plan."

"You are right," Gaius says.

After several days, it is clear that Piso's plan is not going well. Many of Piso's partners have been caught. Many are killed or forced to take their own lives, including Piso. Others are thrown out of Rome.

One morning after Gaius leaves for the Senate, you decide to plan a party for that evening. Many upper-class women host elegant dinner parties for their husbands and important members of Roman society.

You walk outside to your garden to start planning. Soon a slave girl arrives.

The main reception room of a wealthy Roman home was called the atrium.

"You have guests," the girl tells you. She sends three of your closest friends out to the garden.

"We are going to the market," one of the women says. "It's such a lovely summer day. Would you like to join us?"

You're not sure what to do. To host a party tonight requires a lot of planning. But you would also like to spend time with your friends at the market.

➤ To plan the dinner party, turn to page 67.

➤ To go to the market with your friends, turn to page 68.

You decide to stay in Rome. Flavius has denied the charges made against him. You hope Nero will believe Flavius and not his slave.

Several nights later, Roman guards burst into your house and arrest Gaius. He is killed for his part in the plot to kill Nero.

You are lucky to be alive. Many of the plotters are tortured or killed. Some are thrown out of Rome, including Flavius' wife.

You must now choose a new path for your life. A nice man named Marcus wants to marry you. He wants children in order to continue his family line. You could gain even more wealth if you choose to remarry. But as the mother of three children, you have earned your independence. Most widows remarry. But because you are very wealthy, you have more choices.

↠ *To remarry, go to page* **61**

↠ *To stay single, turn to page* **62**

You and Marcus marry and combine your wealth. You stay busy running the household. You go to the Forum to purchase food in the open-air markets. You and your friends go to the public baths, but at different times than the men do.

You soon find out that you're expecting a baby. You feel sick and weak all the time. On the day of the birth, the midwife and your sisters arrive. The birth happens quickly and is very painful. You become weak from loss of blood.

The midwife calls Marcus to your bedside. The last thing you see before your life slips away is your husband's face. You are one of many Roman women who dies in childbirth.

THE END

To follow another path, turn to page 11.
To read the conclusion, turn to page 101.

You turn down Marcus' offer of marriage. You want to manage your own affairs, just as you've seen a few other wealthy women do.

At the market, you meet with other women who are also wealthy and single. Some run their own businesses, such as bakeries and fabric shops. Others use their wealth to sponsor artists.

"I want to do something good with all of my money," you tell the women.

"You can do whatever you want," says one older woman. "Do you like the arts? Or are you more business-minded? Perhaps buying and selling properties would suit you better."

Real estate could help you increase your wealth. But you do enjoy the arts. You like to read poetry, and you love the beautiful sculptures that Roman artists create.

➤ To go into real estate, turn to page **64**.

➤ To support the arts, turn to page **66**.

You and Gaius decide to take the children and leave Rome. But you discover that there is no way out. Nero's guards block every road out of Rome.

You stop a man walking down the street. "Why are the roads closed?" you ask.

"Nero has blockaded the entire city," the man tells you. "He is rounding up those who plotted against him."

You and Gaius exchange nervous glances. It is only a matter of time before you are caught and killed. You wish you had never encouraged your husband to plot against the emperor of Rome.

THE END

To follow another path, turn to page 11.
To read the conclusion, turn to page 101.

Apartments in ancient Rome sat above businesses that opened to the street.

With the money you already have, you buy a small apartment that you will rent out. This apartment is in the center of Rome, in the valley below the hills. This is where the poorer people live. Air quality is poor in the crowded valley. Most Romans cannot afford to buy their own homes. They must rent from people like you.

One day, a man approaches you. "I hear you have an apartment for rent," he says. "I am a shoemaker with a wife and two small children. Is there enough room for my workshop?"

You shake your head. "It's a very small apartment," you say. "But you could move your beds and table to the back of the room during the day. Then you would have enough room for a shop." The shoemaker looks pleased.

You charge him a high rent, as many landlords do. He and his family barely get by. It doesn't take long for you to become richer. You buy more apartments and rent those as well. Soon, you are able to buy a home high on the Palatine hill, where the very richest people live. You are a fine example of a successful Roman woman.

THE END

To follow another path, turn to page 11.
To read the conclusion, turn to page 101.

You find a talented poet to support. You are his patron, and he is your client. Patron-client relationships are common. Patrons give money to clients. The clients run errands for patrons and help manage household affairs. If patrons are active in politics, clients campaign for them.

Clients are usually loyal to their patrons. Your client is no exception. The money you provide allows your client to write poetry without working. In turn, he helps you manage your business affairs.

You live out your years as a well-respected patron. Your client goes on to become a successful poet, thanks to you. When you die, you are buried in a beautiful tomb that bears your name. This honor is very rare for a woman.

THE END

To follow another path, turn to page 11.
To read the conclusion, turn to page 101.

Dinner party guests often took home leftovers in napkins.

You order your slaves to set up a long table in the garden and to prepare the best foods in Rome. The guests arrive a few hours later. Slaves carry trays of meat, vegetables, and pastries. You and your guests lie on benches as you eat pork, shellfish, onions, cabbage, and bread. You eat with your hands and rinse them in bowls of water. A dancer entertains the guests while they eat.

The party lasts long into the evening. You go to bed that night with a smile on your face.

THE END

To follow another path, turn to page 11.
To read the conclusion, turn to page 101.

"The slaves can take care of the planning," you tell your friends. You put on your cloak and walk to the market with your friends. The streets are less crowded in the afternoon, but there still are people everywhere.

The market stalls sit on the ground level of the crowded apartment buildings. Merchants sell items such as food, spices, shoes, and books. You buy some gold jewelry and silk tunics.

On the walk home, you start to feel strange. Your face is hot to the touch. You cancel the party and go to bed early. You wake up in the middle of the night. Your body doubles over with painful cramps as you vomit and have diarrhea.

Gaius is worried. "Could it be Roman fever?" he asks.

You nod your head, too weak to talk. Many people catch Roman fever, especially in the hot summer months. This fever makes people sick with vomiting and diarrhea. You wish you had decided to spend your summer in the countryside. The air is better there. By morning, you are dead.

69

THE END

To follow another path, turn to page 11.
To read the conclusion, turn to page 101.

Constantine was the first Christian emperor of the Roman Empire.

CHAPTER 4

The End of Rome

It is AD 408. Rome is a shell of its former self. The city is no longer the center of the empire. Constantine became emperor in AD 324. He thought Rome was too associated with former emperors. Constantine moved the capital to a city called Byzantium in a Greek region. He renamed it Constantinople, after himself.

The entire Roman Empire is weak. Taxes are very high to support the huge army needed to guard a large number of provinces. As a result, people are becoming poorer. Barbarian tribes outside of the empire are becoming stronger and more organized. They have already attacked several of the empire's provinces. It's only a matter of time before they come to Rome, which has no standing army.

Turn the page.

You are a poor Roman citizen. You work as a carpenter, but you don't make much money. Your diet is made up of bland foods such as bread and porridge.

One day, you look out the window of your cramped apartment. Many people are running in the streets. You go outside to find out what's happening.

"Come quickly!" your neighbor says to you. "Alaric and his troops are approaching the city wall. We must leave now if we hope to escape!"

Alaric is the leader of the Visigoths, a tribe from the North. They once fought for the Roman Army. They want to be paid in land for their service. But the current emperor, Honorius, refuses to meet their demands. If the Visigoths are allowed to take Rome, it could be the end of this great city.

You join a group that is running toward the city wall. Alaric's army is getting closer. There might be time to escape the city.

Rome is nothing like the city it used to be. Old men pass down tales from earlier generations about the glory days of Rome. It's hard for you to believe that the empire was once so powerful. Now, it seems as if every day there's a new story about barbarian invasions throughout the provinces.

Others join you at the wall. One man turns to you and speaks. "I'm going to try to leave the city. I don't think Rome can survive an attack."

Another man speaks. "How will you escape? Alaric's forces will soon surround the city. You could die at the hands of the barbarians."

↬ To try to leave Rome, turn to page 74.

↬ To remain in the city, turn to page 79.

You and others find a gate in the wall. Past the gate is a thick grove of trees that will provide good cover. Perhaps you can wait there until nightfall. Then you can move under the cover of darkness.

You make it safely to the trees. You hear the shouts of men and the hooves of horses approaching the city. You watch the Visigoths pass on the road in front of you. You are thankful they don't see you.

"Where will you go?" you whisper to the man next to you.

"I'm going to try to reach Constantinople," he says. "I've heard it's more stable in the East. The Visigoths are concentrating on the West."

The Visigoths made Alaric their king in AD 395.

You might be safer in Constantinople. But it's hundreds of miles away. The trip there would take weeks. You would have to walk to Brundisium, a town on the coast of southern Italy. Then you would take a ship east through the Mediterranean Sea.

Maybe you can make your way to the countryside. There you could find work as a laborer or a farmer. But if you stay near Rome, you will probably run into Visigoths or other barbarians again.

➤ To flee to the countryside, turn to page **76**.

➤ To go to Constantinople, turn to page **89**.

Ancient Roman farmers grew crops such as wheat, rye, barley, grapes, and olives.

You walk into the countryside and come upon a small farmhouse. You knock at the door, and a man answers.

"I am from Rome," you explain. "It is not safe there. May I stay here?"

The man scratches his chin. "You're welcome here. But you will need to earn your keep." The man shakes your hand. "I'm Tiberius."

Most people in the Roman Empire are farmers. Many people work for rich landowners. You help Tiberius in his grain field. You also help take care of the sheep and goats.

A few days later, Tiberius comes home with news. "Alaric and his troops have left Rome," he tells you. "They took wagons full of gold, silver, silk tunics, and pepper."

This is happy news. Rome is safe once again. But you enjoy your new life on the farm. You decide to stay.

A couple of years pass. It is now AD 410. Emperor Honorius has once again failed to meet Alaric's demand for land.

One day, you and Tiberius go to Rome to buy some new tools for the farm. As you are walking, you spot several Visigoths.

"Well, what have we here?" you hear someone say in a deep voice. You look around. Men in full armor tower over you. "Slaves, maybe? Where did you come from?"

Turn the page.

"We're on our way to Rome," Tiberius says, his voice shaking. "Please don't hurt us."

"Our great leader, Alaric, is now sacking your city." The soldiers look at each other. "What do you say?" one of the Visigoths asks another. "These men look strong. They would be of great use to us as slaves."

More soldiers come down the road and surround you on all sides. You have no choice. You must go with these men wherever they lead you.

They bind your hands and force you to march. It looks as if you're heading to Rome. You will wait there until the Visigoths decide what to do with you next.

78

Turn to page 86

You stay in Rome. If the Romans give Alaric what he wants, perhaps you can avoid bloodshed.

But the conditions quickly turn grim. Alaric and his troops are not letting any food into Rome. Alaric hopes to starve Roman citizens until Emperor Honorius meets his demands of grain, gold, and land. Alaric also calls for the release of all barbarian slaves.

After several days, the city's magistrates tell you to eat less food. As the siege continues, you must eat even less. People are becoming weaker. Many starve to death. Dead bodies line the streets.

Honorius ruled the Western Roman Empire.

Turn the page.

One day, your neighbor comes to your door.

"We must do something. My family will starve. My children are very ill," he says. "I heard that Laeta, the former empress, and her mother, Pissamena, have food. Some of us are planning to break in and steal the food. Will you help us?"

You're also very hungry. But you're not sure if you want to steal. You've heard that the senators are preparing to bargain with Alaric.

"Maybe it's best to wait a day or two," you say. "The senators might reach a deal with Alaric soon."

"I don't think I can wait," your neighbor says. "Food is available now. Let's take this chance."

→ To steal food, go to page 81

→ To wait, turn to page 85

"All right," you say. "Let's go and see what we can find."

You and your neighbor join others who walk to Laeta's house. You hope the rumors are true and that she has a lot of food stored away.

By the time you get there, others have beaten you to the house. To your surprise, the former empress is sharing her food with the hungry. You and your neighbor are given a little bread.

"Please thank the empress for her kindness," you say to one of the empress' slaves. Then you head back toward your apartment.

As you are walking, you make a wrong turn. You are at a dead end. When you turn around, three men block your path. They are thin and dirty.

Turn the page.

"Out all alone, are you?" one of them asks.

"I'm on my way back from Laeta's house. She is handing out food." You show them the bread. Perhaps if you offer them your food, they will leave you alone. But then you will be left with nothing. You aren't sure how much longer you can survive without food.

➤ To offer your food to the hungry group, go to page 83

➤ To keep the food for yourself, turn to page 84

Wealthier ancient Romans cooked food in a kitchen. Smoke escaped through a hole in the roof or a vent in the wall.

"Please, take my food," you offer. "I can go back to the empress' house tomorrow." You hold out the bread.

"Thank you for your kindness," one of the men tells you. He takes your food and shares it with the others. Then they turn and walk back into the city. You are safe, but you still need something to eat. You are too weak to go back to the empress' house. You return to your apartment.

Turn to page 85.

You are too hungry to give away your food. You shove the bread into your mouth. The bread is stale, but it fills your belly.

"You are no better than Alaric," one of the men says. He has a strange look in his eyes.

"I'm sorry," you sputter. But it is too late. One of the men slugs you in the stomach, and you reel back in pain. You crawl on the ground, trying to escape. You wish you had given them your food. You have no way to protect yourself. Finally, one blow to the head knocks you unconscious. Death at the hands of the violent group comes quickly.

THE END

To follow another path, turn to page 11.
To read the conclusion, turn to page 101.

You decide it is safer to stay in your apartment than to wander the streets looking for food. One of your other neighbors is kind enough to share some bread with you.

It is clear that Roman citizens are in danger. The senators send a few citizens to talk to Alaric.

After several days, the citizens come back and speak to the crowd. "Alaric said he would give up his siege on two conditions. First, he wants all the gold, silver, and household goods in the city. He also wants all barbarian slaves to be released to him."

The senators go door to door to collect the goods. You hear that some people are hiding their valuables. You could do the same thing. Maybe you should have escaped when you had the chance. Maybe you still can.

➺ To escape the city with your possessions, turn to page **88**.

➺ To give up your possessions, turn to page **91**.

As you approach Rome, you see thousands of Alaric's troops outside the city walls. A Visigoth soldier ties you and Tiberius to a tree. "We'll come back for you when we've sacked Rome," he says. "As weak as this city is, it probably won't take long."

"We have to try to get out of here," Tiberius whispers.

"How?" You nod toward the large Visigoth who's guarding you.

"We'll have to wait until he nods off. I think I can slip out of these bonds. They are already a little loose."

Several hours pass. You can hear shouts and clashes coming from within the city walls. As the sun sets, your guard falls asleep.

"I'm almost out!" Tiberius whispers. His hands slip free. "Let me untie you." Tiberius loosens the bonds around your wrists.

Just then, the guard wakes up. He looks at both of you with fierceness in his eyes.

You must make a quick decision. Do you run away and hope the guard doesn't catch you? Or do you remain still and try to escape later?

→ To run, turn to page **93**.

→ To escape later, turn to page **96**.

You fill a small bag with some pottery and a few plates. Then you follow a few others to the city wall.

Once the sun goes down, you and the others slip through a gate in the wall. You move quietly at the side of the road, traveling among trees when you can.

The group stops to make a plan.

"Let's go to the East," someone says. "We can try to make it to Constantinople."

Passenger ships did not exist in ancient times. People traveled on cargo ships.

You and the others walk south to the coastal town of Brundisium. There you wait for a ship. Ships cross the Mediterranean Sea regularly. They bring spices, foods, and cloth from the empire's far-flung provinces.

You pay a small fee and board the ship. You sleep on the deck and eat the bread you brought with you. The sea crossing is not too rough.

"We are lucky," one of the old sailors tells you. "I've seen many men die on the water."

Turn the page.

> Constantinople had many bustling markets.

After several days, you reach Constantinople.
It's a glorious, beautiful city. The streets bustle
with people. Trade in the markets is brisk.
You think this is perhaps what Rome used to be
like in the stories you've heard. This is a strong
city. Here you will be safe.

THE END

To follow another path, turn to page 11.
To read the conclusion, turn to page 101.

You hope that if you give up your possessions, Alaric and his gang will leave the city. Maybe then Rome can recover from this famine and sickness. You cling to the possibility that Rome can once again recapture its glory days.

When men come to your door, you throw your household goods into the sacks.

The plan works. Alaric becomes extremely rich with thousands of pounds of gold and silver, silk robes, and spices such as pepper. He leaves the city.

"The port is open!" your neighbor soon reports. "Ships are coming in with grain and food. We can eat again!"

Turn the page.

Eventually, people in Rome get fed. Still, the outlook is bleak. You begin to think that it's only a matter of time before Alaric or another barbarian leader returns. Rome is weak. The entire empire is at risk of an attack.

Your worst fear soon comes true. Alaric returns in August of 410. This time, he wants more than money and possessions. He wants to take Rome. For three days, he and his troops plunder the city. Rome is overrun by the Visigoths. The great city has finally has fallen. The Visigoths are in charge. Being a Roman citizen now means nothing.

THE END

To follow another path, turn to page 11.
To read the conclusion, turn to page 101.

"Let's make a run for it!" you shout to Tiberius. Both of you are fast. You easily outrun the guard.

"Where should we go?" Tiberius asks.

"The farm seems like a safe place," you say. "The Visigoths are concerned with Rome."

But Rome used to be your home. If you go back, you could help your family and friends.

➤ To return to the farm, turn to page **94**.

➤ To go to Rome, turn to page **95**.

"Let's return to the farm," you say to Tiberius. Your legs ache and you can barely breathe by the time you reach the farm. The Visigoths did not follow you. You are safe.

You wish the same could be said for the citizens of Rome. For three days, Alaric and his troops plunder the city. They steal everything they can find. They even set a few buildings on fire. Then they leave the once-great city.

You live the rest of your life on the farm. But you wish you had done something to help. Alaric's men killed some of your family and friends. You'll live with that guilt the rest of your life.

THE END

To follow another path, turn to page 11.
To read the conclusion, turn to page 101.

You and Tiberius head to Rome. In the confusion, you are able to slip through one of the gates and into the city. You and Tiberius go straight to the Forum. Visigoth soldiers are raiding the buildings. A group of Roman citizens is attacking them with swords. But the Romans are quickly losing the fight.

"Help us!" one of the Romans yells at you.

Another Roman grabs your arm. "Rome will not win this fight. You should hide in a church. Alaric will spare anyone who hides there."

You aren't sure what to do. You want to help drive the Visigoths out of Rome. But perhaps you should hide in a church for now.

→ To hide in a church, turn to page **97**.

→ To stay and fight, turn to page **98**.

Tiberius runs away, but you feel frozen in place.

The guard sees that you are untied. He grabs the loose bonds and ties you up. The bonds are so tight your wrists bleed.

You stay tied to the tree for three days. You're given little food to eat. One day, the guard unties you from the tree.

"You'll be working on one of our farms in the countryside." The guard ties your hands and roughly shoves you forward.

You wish you had escaped when you had the chance. You have gone from Roman citizen to slave. You will spend the rest of your days in service to the Visigoths.

THE END

To follow another path, turn to page 11.
To read the conclusion, turn to page 101.

You and Tiberius hide in the nearest church. Hundreds of other Romans are also crammed inside the church.

"Are we really safe here?" you ask Tiberius.

"Time will tell," he says.

After plundering Rome for three days, Alaric and his troops leave the city. You and the others step out of the church. Bodies lie dead in the streets. A few buildings are on fire. You are alive, but your city is in shambles. This is a sad day for the once-mighty Roman Empire.

97

THE END

To follow another path, turn to page 11.
To read the conclusion, turn to page 101.

You see a sword lying on the ground. It must belong to someone who has already died. You pick it up and advance toward the Visigoth soldiers.

You find a soldier whose back is turned toward you. You sink the sword into his side. He reels back in pain and falls to the ground. You attack several Visigoths in the same way. Other Roman citizens are doing the same thing. You feel a rush of excitement. Perhaps Rome can be saved after all.

Suddenly, you feel a sharp pain in your neck. You look up, and a Visigoth soldier is grinning at you. You bring your hand to your neck. When you pull your hand away, your fingers are covered in blood.

Alaric and the Visigoths left behind any household gold and silver that was used for religious purposes.

The world starts to turn dark. You will not live to see another day. You can only hope that your fellow Roman citizens can overcome Alaric and the Visigoths. Otherwise, Rome is doomed.

THE END

To follow another path, turn to page 11.
To read the conclusion, turn to page 101.

Emperor Romulus (far right) surrendered to Odoacer (on horse). Odoacer was a German who once served with the Roman Army.

CHAPTER 5

Ancient Rome

The Roman Empire lasted for roughly 1,000 years. It is considered one of the world's greatest civilizations. At its peak, the empire included much of Europe, the Middle East, and northern Africa. Wealth in the form of valuable coins and jewels flooded Rome.

Historians often mark the year AD 476 as the end of the Roman Empire. That year the last emperor of the Western Roman Empire, Romulus Augustulus, was forced from the throne by Odoacer, a barbarian leader. Former provinces such as Gaul and Britannia became separate kingdoms. The eastern part of the empire became known as the Byzantine Empire. Constantinople was its capital. The Byzantine Empire lasted until 1453.

Romans were known for their skills in engineering, public speaking, arts, and architecture. Many ancient Roman buildings still exist. In Rome, people visit the remains of the Colosseum, various temples, and the Forum. Many museums around the world display statues and pottery from ancient Rome.

Remains of the Roman Forum still stand today.

The ruins yield clues as to what life was like in ancient Rome. Some written records also exist. But most written records were left by wealthy, educated male citizens. Historians have little firsthand knowledge about the lives of common people in Rome. But they can determine facts about their lives by examining what was left behind in the ruins.

The ways of ancient Rome continue to influence people today. The creators of the U.S. Constitution looked to the ancient Roman Republic for ideas. Rome's network of magistrates, senators, and consuls worked closely with one another. The creators of the Constitution borrowed this concept of "checks and balances."

People study the essays and speeches of talented Roman writers and public speakers such as Cicero, Seneca, and Julius Caesar. Today's methods of observation and experimentation in the medical field can be traced back to Galen. This Greek doctor treated Roman emperors and gladiators.

The Colosseum was used for gladiator contests, animal hunts, and pretend naval battles. People still visit the Colosseum today.

More than 1,500 years after its fall, ancient Rome continues to fascinate people. In many ways, the people of ancient Rome have much in common with people of today. Roman citizens shopped, made laws, and had close-knit families. They entertained themselves at chariot races and gladiator games, much as people today visit sports stadiums. They lived through times of war and hardship. Above all, they did what they could to survive.

Time Line

753 BC — Date traditionally considered to be the founding of Rome.

509 BC — Ancient Rome changes from a monarchy to a republic.

390 BC — Rome is sacked by the Gauls, a group of people from present-day Western Europe.

378 BC — The Servian Wall is built. It is the first wall to surround the city of Rome.

312 BC — Construction begins on Rome's first aqueduct.

289 BC — Rome produces its first coins.

264 BC — The first gladiator contest is held in Rome.

218–202 BC — Hannibal, a general from the North African city of Carthage, invades Italy from Spain. More than 100,000 Romans are killed during the 16 years of war.

161 BC — Greek philosophers are thrown out of Rome in an effort to remove foreigners and their ideas.

44–30 BC — Rome suffers a civil war that begins with the murder of Julius Caesar. Octavian, Mark Antony, and Lepidus take power.

27 BC — Rome shifts from a republic to a monarchy when Octavian becomes emperor.

AD 64 — Rome suffers a devastating fire that burns for nearly a week. The fire destroys more than two-thirds of the city. Emperor Nero rebuilds the city with stolen money from the provinces.

AD 80 — Rome's Colosseum is dedicated.

AD 166 — Rome and much of the empire suffers from a devastating plague brought by troops returning from the East.

AD 293 — Emperor Diocletian splits the Roman Empire in half. The western half is ruled from Rome. The eastern half is ruled from Nicomedia, in present-day Turkey.

AD 324 — Emperor Constantine becomes the sole ruler of the Roman Empire. He moves the capital of the empire from Rome to Constantinople, in present-day Turkey.

AD 408 — Visigoths, led by Alaric, lay siege to Rome. They return in 410 and sack the city for three days.

AD 476 — The Roman Empire ends when Romulus Augustulus, the emperor of the Western Empire, is forced from the throne. Its provinces become separate kingdoms. The Eastern Empire becomes the Byzantine Empire.

OTHER PATHS TO EXPLORE

In this book, you've seen how the events experienced in ancient Rome look different from three points of view.

Perspectives on history are as varied as the people who lived it. You can explore other paths on your own to learn more about what happened. Seeing history from many points of view is an important part of understanding it.

Here are some ideas for other ancient Rome points of view to explore:

+ Gladiators were usually slaves, criminals, or prisoners of war. They were made to fight to the death, all in front of a large crowd. What was life like for them?

+ Slaves helped wealthy Romans run their land and households. They had very little control over their daily lives. What would it have been like to be a slave in a wealthy Roman household?

+ Emperors had the ultimate power in the Roman Empire. What would it have been like to rule the empire?

Read More

James, Simon. *Eyewitness Ancient Rome.* New York: DK Pub., 2008.

Saunders, Nicholas. *The Life of Julius Caesar.* Columbus, Ohio: School Specialty Pub., 2006.

Sonneborn, Liz. *The Romans: Life in Ancient Rome.* Minneapolis: Millbrook Press, 2010.

Stewart, David. *You Wouldn't Want to be a Roman Soldier!: Barbarians You'd Rather Not Meet.* New York: Franklin Watts, 2006.

Internet Sites

FactHound offers a safe, fun way to find Internet sites related to this book. All of the sites on FactHound have been researched by our staff.

Here's all you do:

Visit *www.facthound.com*

FactHound will fetch the best sites for you!

Glossary

aqueduct (AK-wuh-duhkt) — a large bridge built to carry water across a valley

barbarian (bar-BAYR-ee-uhn) — any one of a number of tribes that invaded the Roman Empire

blockade (blok-AYD) — to close off an area in order to keep people or supplies from going in or out

dowry (DOU-ree) — money or property that women in some cultures bring with them when they marry

empire (EM-pyr) — a large territory ruled by a powerful leader

magistrate (MAJ-uh-strate) — an elected official of ancient Rome

ochre (OH-kuhr) — a type of red or yellow iron ore once used as makeup by men and women in ancient times

plunder (PLUHN-duhr) — to steal things by force

province (PROV-uhnss) — a country or region under the control of the ancient Roman government

republic (ree-PUHB-lik) — a form of government in which the people elect their leaders; two men called consuls headed the Roman Republic.

siege (SEEJ) — the surrounding of a city by troops to cut off supplies and then wait for those inside to surrender

BIBLIOGRAPHY

Adkins, Lesley, and Roy A. Adkins. *Handbook to Life in Ancient Rome*. New York: Facts on File, 2004.

Andreau, Jean. *Banking and Business in the Roman World*. New York: Cambridge University Press, 1999.

Casson, Lionel. *Everyday Life in Ancient Rome*. Baltimore: The Johns Hopkins University Press, 1998.

Casson, Lionel. *Travel in the Ancient World*. Baltimore: Johns Hopkins University Press, 1994.

Gardner, Jane F. *Women in Roman Law and Society*. Bloomington, Ind.: Indiana University Press, 1986.

Goldsworthy, Adrian. *Caesar: Life of a Colossus*. New Haven, Conn.: Yale University Press, 2006.

Mitchell, Stephen. *A History of the Later Roman Empire, AD 284-641: The Transformation of the Ancient World*. Malden, Mass.: Blackwell, 2007.

Parenti, Michael. *The Assassination of Julius Caesar: A People's History of Ancient Rome*. New York: New Press, 2003.

INDEX